The Grammar *of* SPICE

Wrapping Paper with Gift Tags

10 SHEETS + 12 TAGS

Thames & Hudson

Designed by Here Design

First published in 2018 in the
United States of America by
Thames & Hudson Inc.,
500 Fifth Avenue,
New York, New York 10110

www.thamesandhudsonusa.com

ISBN 978-0-500-42091-1

Printed and manufactured in China

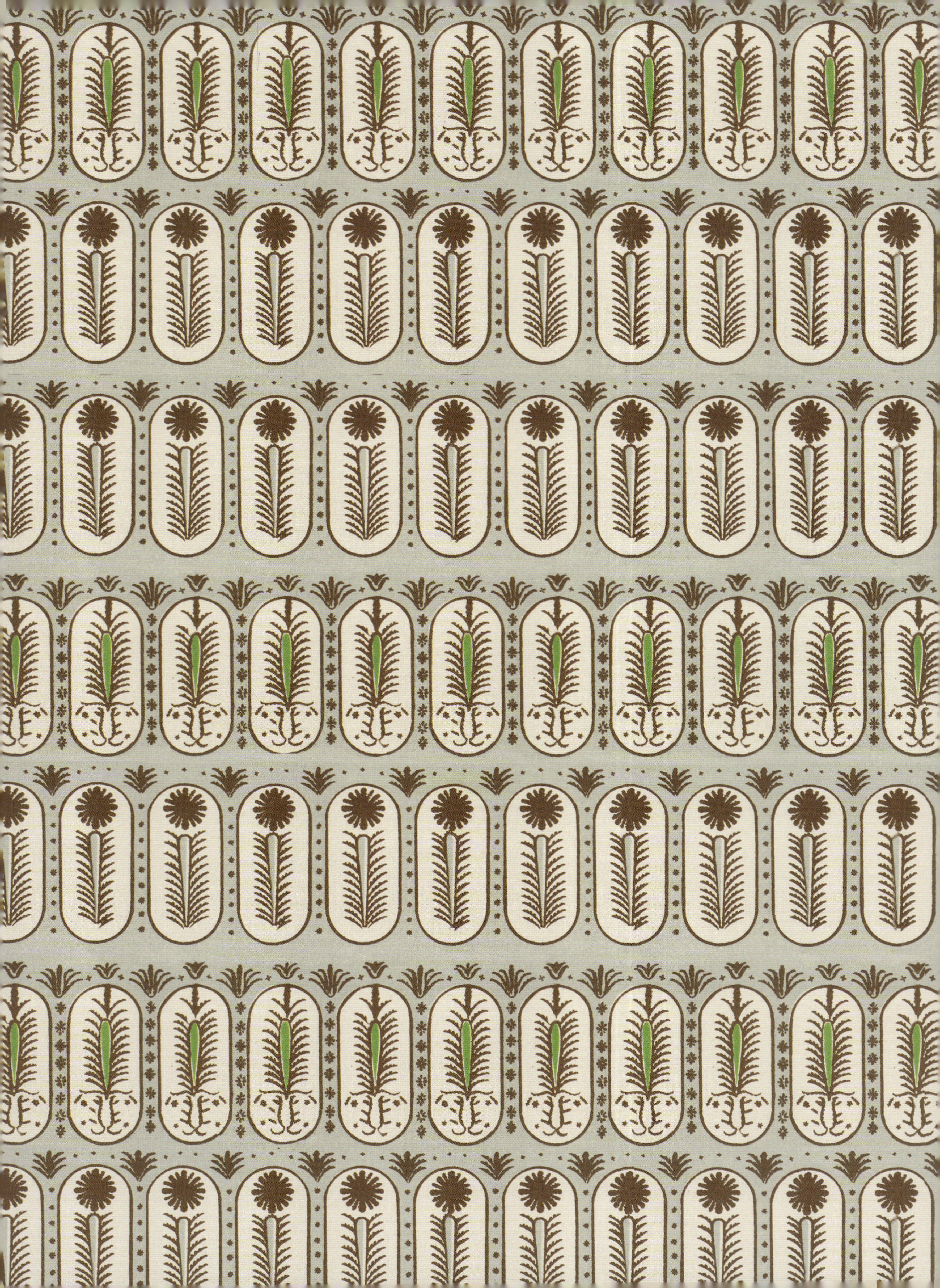